NUESTRA AMERICA

NUESTRA AMÉRICA

NATIONAL MUSEUM *of the*
AMERICAN LATINO
Smithsonian

NUESTRA AMÉRICA

30 INSPIRING LATINAS/LATINOS WHO HAVE SHAPED THE UNITED STATES

BY SABRINA VOURVOULIAS
ILLUSTRATED BY GLORIA FÉLIX

Introduction by Eduardo Díaz, Deputy Director
National Museum of the American Latino

Reading Guide by Emily Key, Office of Audience Engagement,
National Museum of the American Latino

SCHOLASTIC INC.

ISBN 978-1-338-87852-3

12 11 10 9 8 7 6 5 4 3 2 1   23 24 25 26 27 28

Printed in the U.S.A.   40

First Scholastic printing, January 2023

Cover and interior design by Frances J. Soo Ping Chow

TABLE OF CONTENTS

Dear Reader,

Latinas and Latinos—native born and immigrant—have played and continue to play foundational roles in nation-building and the shaping of our national culture as patriots, educators, entrepreneurs, laborers, artists, healers, innovators, entertainers, scientists, community activists, and leaders. Since its inception in 1997, the Smithsonian Latino Center supported ongoing research, exhibitions, collecting, public and educational programs, digital content, and publications that interpret and illustrate the diverse Latino experience in the United States.

Nuestra América was inspired by the National Museum of the American Latino's effort to center Latino stories as part of the greater American narrative through the building of the Molina Family Latino Gallery. This gallery fulfills a promise and vision set decades earlier—before the National Museum of the American Latino was established. The Molina Gallery's exhibitions will present stories on many, if not most, of the remarkable Americans featured throughout this book. History is largely made by people, and it is through their life stories that we will be able to paint a more accurate portrait of our country's past, present, and future. Latino history is American history.

This publication marks a groundbreaking moment in the Smithsonian's history. I can think of no better way to enter the world of youth literature than by collaborating on a publication that showcases thirty illustrious Latiras and Latinos and their impactful contributions. Through these pages, you will learn about the trials, tribulations, and ultimate successes of these individuals in the fields of entertainment, social and environmental justice, sports, education, fashion design, journalism, aviation, literature, politics, space exploration, LGBTQ advocacy, health care, entrepreneurship, music, science, and military service, just to name a few. Limiting our choices to thirty individuals among a bounty of notable figures was incredibly difficult. Our hope is that you will see these profiles as an initial exploration and will go on to learn about many others in the Latino community who have made and continue to make meaningful contributions to strengthening the fabric of this country.

We are immensely grateful to our colleagues at Hachette Group/Running Press Kids and Smithsonian Enterprises for believing in our work and extending this wonderful opportunity to us. Special thanks to Jill Corcoran at Smithsonian Enterprises and Emily Key at the National Museum of the American Latino for their vision and leadership on this project. A thank you to Adrián Aldaba and Natalia Febo at the Latino Museum for their efforts in completing this project.

The great labor leader César Chávez once said, "We cannot seek achievement for ourselves and forget about progress and prosperity of our community. . . . Our ambitions must be broad enough to include the aspirations and needs of others, for their sake and for our own." I hope that you are inspired by the sense of community that guided the ambitions and propelled the achievements of these distinguished Latina and Latino Americans. In closing, I hope you are moved to set your personal goals high and to always be one with your communities and their needs and aspirations. Keep your eyes on the prize!

Atentamente,
Eduardo Díaz, Deputy Director
National Museum of the American Latino
www.latino.si.edu

NUESTRA AMÉRICA

SYLVIA ACEVEDO

(circa 1957–)

ENGINEER

Sylvia remembers being a child and looking up at the night sky. She was in the Girl Scouts, and they were camping out, eating s'mores, and relaxing after a day of outdoor activities. The troop leader noticed Sylvia looking up at the sky, so she pointed out the planets and the constellations. It was the first time Sylvia understood what those twinkling lights really were. Soon enough, Sylvia tried to earn her Girl Scout science badge by launching a rocket. Both rockets and Girl Scouts would end up being a part of Sylvia's future. But first she'd have to learn to believe in herself.

Sylvia was born in South Dakota but grew up in the desert landscape of Las Cruces, New Mexico. Her mother was a Mexican immigrant, and her father was Mexican American and from El Paso, Texas. They spoke Spanish at home and didn't have a lot of money. Sylvia's mother noticed that the kids from their neighborhood (which had dirt streets) seemed to get sick more than the kids from other neighborhoods, so when Sylvia's sister got sick with meningitis, they moved. Sylvia didn't like leaving her friends behind, but she soon found her place when she joined the Girl Scouts.

Besides teaching her about the night sky, Sylvia's troop leader taught her never to walk away from a cookie sale until she'd heard no three times. Sylvia used this technique when she was a senior in high school. "Girls like you don't go to college," the high school counselor told her. Sylvia walked into the counselor's office anyway. The exasperated counselor asked her what she wanted to study. When Sylvia said, "Engineering," the counselor burst into laughter. But Sylvia went on to get her industrial engineering degree from New Mexico State University in 1979. She became a rocket scientist at NASA's jet propulsion lab where

"I LOVE NUMBERS. NUMBERS ARE SORT OF MY SUPERPOWER."

she worked on the *Voyager* mission that flew by Jupiter and its moons.

Then she went back to school and got her master's degree at Stanford University. She had wanted to go there ever since her fourth-grade teacher showed her a photo of the university. There, she became one of the first Latinas to earn a graduate-level engineering degree.

As a systems engineer, she decided to get into tech. There weren't as many women as men in that industry in the 1980s, and at one of her jobs, there wasn't even a bathroom for her to use. Sylvia thought maybe they hoped she'd quit her job because of the inconvenience. Instead, Sylvia brought a bike to work and rode it to the nearest bathroom.

When the company finally realized she was the type of person who would solve a problem instead of walking away from it, they installed a Porta Potty for her. Sylvia worked for some of the biggest names in tech—IBM, Dell, and Apple—and became a tech entrepreneur. But she never forgot the impact the Girl Scouts had on her life.

She joined the Girl Scouts' board of directors and eventually became the CEO. Since she has headed the organization, the Girl Scouts have added robotics, coding, engineering, and cybersecurity to the badges girls can earn—while continuing to teach them the persistence and resilience Sylvia has found so valuable in her own life.

Way back when she was working on her science badge trying to launch her rocket, Sylvia needed to figure out how to break gravity's grip to successfully get her rocket off the ground. Now Sylvia is working to help others break the grip on whatever is holding them down. She's written a book, *Path to the Stars: My Journey from Girl Scout to Rocket Scientist*, to inspire middle school girls to believe in themselves and their ambitions.

After all, a Girl Scout is taught to always leave the campground—and the world—better than how she found it.

LUIS WALTER ÁLVAREZ

(1911–1988)

PHYSICIST

Friends and coworkers of Luis Álvarez would sometimes open the door to his office at the University of California, Berkeley, and catch him doing a handstand on top of his desk. Not exactly what you'd expect from a Nobel prize–winning physicist, but then, Luis seemed to enjoy standing things on their heads.

Born in San Francisco in 1911, Luis—known as Luie (*loo-ee*) to his friends—was the son of a physician. He was named after his Spanish grandfather, who was also a physician, but Luie had no interest in medicine. He liked to tinker—he built a radio when he was eleven years old—and during high school he spent two summers apprenticing in the instrument shop of the Mayo Clinic in Rochester, Minnesota. This affection for tinkering stayed with Luie, and over the course of his life, he was granted twenty-two patents—for everything from optical devices to a golf training machine developed for President Eisenhower.

After high school, Luie enrolled in the University of Chicago in 1928 to study chemistry. He was a B student, and in his junior year, he switched

to physics instead. He took twelve physics courses in eighteen months to make up for his late start in the subject and reportedly read every nuclear physics article that had ever been published. Later, friends would remember that when he quoted an article he had read, he could recollect every detail about it, including whether it appeared on the left-hand or right-hand page of the journal.

"ACTUALLY, PHYSICS IS THE SIMPLEST OF ALL SCIENCES."

He loved physics, insisting that it was a simple science complicated only by the language physicists used to discuss it—the language of mathematics. Luie also loved airplanes (he had a pilot's license and flew until he was seventy-three), which led him to invent a radar-based system that allowed aircraft to land safely in fog and at night. The military thought this and some of Luie's other inventions could help the United States during World War I. He was one of a number of scientists who were part of the Manhattan Project, which developed the atomic bombs dropped on Japan during World War II.

But his peacetime projects also gained recognition. In 1968, Luie was awarded the Nobel Prize in Physics for the use of liquid hydrogen in a bubble chamber with which he discovered many short-lived sub-atomic particles.

Late in life, after he had officially retired from doing research, Luie had the time to use physics to solve mysteries that captured the public's imagination. For example, he used cosmic rays to help archaeologists figure out if the chambers underneath one of the Egyptian pyramids were empty or full without having to dig the chambers out (they were empty, alas). Working with his geologist son, Walt, he was the first to say that the impact of a massive asteroid had been the cause of the mass extinction of dinosaurs. Many paleontologists initially rejected his asteroid theory. It wasn't until after Luie's death in 1988 that an impact crater large enough to uphold such a theory was discovered, making it accepted as the most likely cause of the extinction event.

Throughout his life, Luie happily followed his father's guidance: "He advised me to sit every few months in my reading chair for an entire evening, close my eyes, and try to think of new problems to solve."

PURA BELPRÉ

(1899–1982)

LIBRARIAN AND STORYTELLER

Since 1996, her face has appeared on a round, golden seal marking the books of Latino writers and illustrators who are honored for their work on an outstanding work of literature for children and youth. The Pura Belpré Award, cosponsored by three national library organizations, would have delighted Pura, who was, in 1921, the first Puerto Rican hired by the New York Public Library system. (Some say she was very likely the first Puerto Rican librarian in the mainland United States.)

"I SAID TO MYSELF I AM GOING TO DO SOMETHING WITH THESE STORIES."

An Afro-Latina, Pura was hired to work at the 135th Street branch in Harlem, where there was a growing population of Puerto Ricans, many of them black. "One of my duties in the children's room was to 'read' the fairy tale shelves," Pura wrote later in life. "Thus the folklore of the world opened for me. As I shelved books, I searched for some of the folktales I had heard at home. There was not even one. A sudden feeling of loss rose within me."

So she decided to write her own retellings of traditional Puerto Rican folktales. Her tale of a mouse and cockroach that fall in love, *Pérez y Martina*, was published in 1932 and was the first Spanish-language book for children published by a mainstream U.S. publisher. She would go on to write other children's books and a collection of Puerto Rican folktales.

Pura didn't start out thinking she'd become a librarian, folklorist, and storyteller. Born in Cidra, Puerto Rico, to a middle-class family that moved a lot because of her father's work as a building contractor, Pura graduated from high school in Santurce intending to go to college to become a teacher. Instead, after one year at the University of Puerto Rico, she went to New York City to help her sister plan her wedding—and decided to stay.

At first, like many other Puerto Rican women who migrated from the island at that time, she toiled as a garment worker. Pura was offered the library assistant job—thanks to her education and the library's need for her Spanish-language skills—after her newlywed sister turned it down. Some historians have noted that Pura had more liberty than most young Puerto Rican women of her time to pursue this opportunity because she wasn't living under the supervision of parents, nor was she married with children.

In addition to doing the typical work of an assistant librarian, Pura presented puppet shows in English and Spanish. Pura considered the library the jewel of the community. Her time there, she would later say, was especially rewarding. "It acquainted me with Black culture and I experienced the Black Renaissance of art and literature, and the upsurge of poets, novelists, dramatists, and musicians. I saw the beginning of the now Schomburg collection come into being."

In fact, Arturo Schomburg—the Black Puerto Rican historian whose collection of literature, art, and narratives form the basis of the Schomburg Center for Research in Black Culture's holdings—used to come to the library and chat with Pura.

At forty, Pura married Clarence Cameron White, an African American violinist and composer (whose papers are now part of the Schomburg collection), and they resided in Harlem throughout their marriage.

She left the 135th Street branch after several years to work at the 115th Street branch, which would become an important cultural center for Latino residents of the city. There, she arranged for famed Mexican muralist Diego Rivera to lecture, celebrated Latino feast days, and honed her storytelling and puppetry skills. She later worked at the 110th Street branch before "retiring" to concentrate on writing her books.

After her husband's death in 1960, she came out of retirement to work again at the New York Public Library, this time in the South Bronx. She died in 1982, but her legendary status as a storyteller lives on in the award named after her. To this day, Teatro SEA (a Latinx children's theater in New York) sends its actresses out to perform puppet shows at schools dressed up as Pura.

MARTHA E. BERNAL

(1931–2001)

CLINICAL PSYCHOLOGIST

She would go on to become the first Latina in the nation to earn a doctorate in psychology, but the first thing Martha Bernal learned when she got to kindergarten was that, if she spoke Spanish, she'd be punished by the teacher. Later, after she became a groundbreaking psychologist, she would remember the shame this made her feel.

"In 1939, when I began school in El Paso, Texas, the use of the Spanish language by Mexican children was punished in Texas schools," Martha wrote in 1988. "Because I did not speak English, I immediately learned that the dominant society disapproved of my language and heritage."

Martha was born in San Antonio, Texas, to Alicia and Enrique de Bernal, who had recently immigrated from Mexico, and was raised in El Paso, where schools were segregated and Mexican Americans experienced significant discrimination. Her family was tight-knit and traditional, which gave her a strong connection to her identity but presented some difficulties, as well.

When Martha graduated from high school and told her father she wanted to go to college, he objected. He wanted her to get married and start a family. Finally, with her mother's and sister's intercession, he relented. "My father gave in and assisted me financially even though . . . I knew it was economically difficult for him to help," she wrote in 1988.

She completed her bachelor's degree at the University of Texas, got a master's degree from Syracuse University, and then went on to get a doctorate in clinical psychology from Indiana University in 1962, becoming the first Latina to do so.

"I HAVE MUCH TO LEARN AND MANY THINGS LEFT TO ACCOMPLISH."

She and her female peers experienced sexism while completing their studies. At first, professors tried to dissuade Martha from taking "difficult" courses like advanced mathematics, and later, she saw that women students were not invited to work on research projects with their professors. When Martha started applying for faculty jobs, she experienced sexism again. More than once, she heard the words "We do not hire women."

Described by her friends as resilient, passionate, and outspoken against injustice, Martha didn't let the rejections distract her from what she wanted to accomplish. She became a researcher, focusing her work on how behavioral treatments worked on children.

At the same time, she found herself confronting some of the anti-Latino racism she had internalized from her childhood in El Paso. This led her to focus the research she was doing on the treatment of mental health issues in children of color. Because she saw few Latinos working in her field, she made it her priority to make recruitment more multicultural and encouraged Latino students to study psychology.

Her persistence and belief in herself and her cultural traditions made her a trailblazer.

Martha died in 2001, but not before inspiring a whole new generation of Latino psychologists.

JULIA DE BURGOS

(1914–1953)

POET

"I AM LIFE, STRENGTH, WOMAN."

In a letter written to her sister when she first arrived in New York, Julia de Burgos wrote: "I want to be universal." Though she died at the young age of thirty-nine, the Puerto Rican poet and advocate for Puerto Rico's independence achieved her dream.

There are monuments to her in Puerto Rico; a street named after her in East Harlem; schools named after her in New York, Philadelphia, Chicago, and Puerto Rico; postage stamps that commemorate her in the United States and the Dominican Republic; and countless murals and artworks that celebrate her as a poet, feminist, and Afro-Latina trailblazer.

She was born Julia Constanza Burgos García in Carolina, Puerto Rico. Julia was the eldest of her thirteen siblings, seven of whom died in childhood. The family was working-class, and she attended college on a scholarship, graduating with a teaching certificate at the age of nineteen.

She accomplished a lot very quickly: She took a job at a social service site that offered free meals to poor children, got married, took on her first teaching job at Naranjito, Puerto Rico, joined the Daughters of Liberty nationalist political group, and wrote two children's plays—all by the age of twenty-two.

Traditionally, when women married in Latin America, they would take on their husband's surname and insert a "de" before it to indicate whom they "belonged" to. When Julia divorced her husband three years after marrying him, she inserted a "de" before her own surname to indicate she would belong to no one but herself.

Julia self-published her first book of poetry, which contained one of her most enduringly beloved poems, "Río Grande de Loíza," in which the river is personified and its waters have become the tears of the enslaved Puerto Rican people.

Located on the coastal northeast of the island, the Loíza region that the Río Grande traverses has a significant Black population and is acknowledged as a place where African and Taíno Indigenous traditions are alive in music, folk art, and cuisine. By setting the poem where she did, Julia found a way to decry the island's history of slavery and its colonial occupation, first by Spain and then by the United States.

Though there are no remaining copies of Julia's self-published first book, "Río Grande de Loíza" was included in her second book of poems—published in 1939, this time by a traditional publisher—and earned her both acclaim and an avid readership. Even though poetry opened some doors for her, as a divorced woman in a fiercely Catholic country, and because of her African descent and working-class background, she found herself only marginally accepted by the intellectual circles on the island.

Julia moved to New York City in 1940 as politics on the island veered away from the independence movement she believed in, and she swore she'd never return. Poignantly, for the woman who wanted to be universal, when she collapsed on a corner of East Harlem in 1953, she had no identification on her and was declared a Jane Doe when she died that same day. The city buried her as a nameless indigent in a public burial site.

After weeks of searching, her family and friends finally found her body, had it exhumed, and flew her remains to her hometown in Puerto Rico, where she was formally buried with a grand monument erected in her memory.

Not counting the self-published book, Julia had seen two of her books of poetry published during her lifetime; a third would be published posthumously in 1954. But even with such limited poetic output, she has come to be considered one of the most influential Puerto Rican and Latin American poets of the twentieth century.

CÉSAR CHÁVEZ

(1927–1993)

LABOR ORGANIZER

‖‖‖‖‖‖‖‖‖‖‖‖‖‖‖‖‖‖‖‖‖‖‖‖‖‖‖‖‖

"IF YOU WANT TO REMEMBER ME, ORGANIZE!"

‖‖‖‖‖‖‖‖‖‖‖‖‖‖‖‖‖‖‖‖‖‖‖‖‖‖‖‖‖

More than fifty thousand mourners were at the funeral of César Chávez, a Mexican American with an unshakeable belief in nonviolent change who helped launch the farmworkers' movement in the United States.

César was born in Yuma, Arizona, and learned early about injustice when his father was swindled out of the family's house and lands. The family moved to California, and César's father worked the fields in McFarland, Delano, and Salinas, among many other places. César and his brother Richard attended thirty-seven different schools as a result.

César had completed his schooling through the eighth grade when his father was in an accident, so César went to work in the fields to support the family. When he was nineteen, he enlisted in the U.S. Navy and served for two years. After returning to civilian life, he married Helen Fabela, with whom he would have eight children, and settled down in Delano.

A devout Catholic who took to heart the faith's social teachings, César was outraged by the conditions faced by farmworkers in Delano: they worked long hours in the fields, in poor conditions (they had no toilets to use, for example), and for very little pay, which was sometimes withheld from them. They even had to pay the growers to live in metal shacks with no water or electricity just to be close to the fields they picked.

César became an organizer at the Community Service Organization before founding the National Farm Workers Association in 1962 with Dolores Huerta. They worked to set up a credit union and a cooperative gas station for farmworkers, as well as to create a way for farmworker families to receive death benefits if a tragedy occurred in the fields.

In September 1965, the Farm Workers Association voted to join a strike led by the Filipino Agricultural Workers Organizing Committee in the grape fields of Delano. In 1966, César led a 340-mile march from Delano to Sacramento that drew national attention.

The Latino and Filipino associations merged around this time and became the United Farm Workers (UFW), with César as its director and Larry Itliong as its assistant director. Both men were at the table in 1970 when twenty-six Delano growers signed a contract with the UFW that secured higher pay and benefits for ten thousand farmworkers. "Once social change begins, it cannot be reversed," César said.

He was committed to ensuring that the farmworker movement was a nonviolent one. His first hunger strike, in 1968, was expressly concerned with getting UFW members to commit formally to keeping the movement nonviolent. The fast lasted twenty-five days, brought national attention to the farmworker cause, and prompted Martin Luther King Jr. to send him a telegram expressing his solidarity.

His last hunger strike in 1988—protesting the use of pesticides in table grapes and reviving interest in a four-year consumer boycott of them—lasted thirty-six days. When he ended his fast, celebrities and activists took up where he left off, among them the Reverends Jesse Jackson and J. Lowery as well as actors Martin Sheen, Emilio Estévez, Edward James Olmos, Danny Glover, and Whoopi Goldberg.

César was awarded a posthumous Medal of Freedom from President Bill Clinton in 1994, and in 2014, President Barack Obama issued a federal commemorative proclamation, which enables states to celebrate César's birthday, March 31, as a holiday.

The man with an eighth-grade education, who never made more than $5,000 a year, who had unshakable faith in the dignity of all human beings, and who was willing to put his own body on the line to safeguard farmworkers' rights, built a movement that outlived him. The UFW carries on his legacy to this day.

"However important the struggle is and however much misery, poverty, and exploitation exist," César would say, "we know that it cannot be more important than one human life."

SANDRA CISNEROS

(1954—)

AUTHOR

Sandra Cisneros was born in Chicago, one of seven children and the only daughter of a Mexican father and a Chicana* mother. Growing up with six brothers was noisy—"the library was the first place I found that was quiet"—and when Sandra went to the library and read books, she says she found a place made for thinking and the imagination.

That thinking and imagination led to her writing two novels, a collection of short stories, two full-length poetry books, a picture book for adults, a children's book, a book of essays—and she hasn't finished yet.

The household Sandra grew up in was bicultural and bilingual, and the family frequently traveled back and forth between Mexico and the United States. She has said that gave her double the words to use when writing. In public appearances, while often dressed in the colorful *rebozos* and elaborately worked *huipiles* native to certain regions of Mexico, she switches effortlessly from English to Spanish and back again as she speaks.

Sandra's presentations leave audiences feeling empowered by her example and awed by her imagination. Ironically, one of Sandra's elementary school teachers complained that she was a daydreamer—something the teacher clearly didn't think was positive but has undoubtedly helped fuel Sandra's creativity.

She wrote poetry in high school and was the literary magazine editor before going on to earn her bachelor's degree in English from Loyola University of Chicago in 1976. She has said, however, that it wasn't until she was at the University of Iowa getting her master's degree that she found her voice as a writer.

"WHAT I'M SAYING IN MY WRITING IS THAT WE CAN BE LATINO AND STILL BE AMERICAN."

The House on Mango Street, Sandra's first published novel (1984), was written from the perspective of a Latina teen and was the first time many readers had seen themselves represented on the page. It has become wildly successful—selling over six million copies, being translated into twenty languages, and becoming required reading in elementary schools and high schools across the nation.

Sandra has worked as a teacher, a college recruiter, an arts administrator, and an artist in the schools where she taught creative writing. In her interactions with young people, she came to understand that her greatest impact on their lives might be as a writer because "if you don't see yourself reflected in a story, you can't imagine you can make any difference in the world."

Building community is a profound part of Sandra's work. She was an integral part of the cultural community of San Antonio, where she lived for many years. While she has received many awards for her writing (including a National Medal of the Arts), the MacArthur Genius Fellowship she received in 1995 enabled her to start the Macondo Foundation—an important support for socially engaged writers. She is also the founder of the Alfredo Cisneros Del Moral Foundation, which gives grants to writers from Texas.

"Can art save lives? That is the question I asked myself in my twenties," she said in a Ford Foundation video. Her life echoes the answer that brings that video to a close: "Art does change us for the better."

(*Chicano/Chicana—The term to describe Mexican Americans born and raised in the United States who actively celebrate Mexican culture and Indigenous roots but are, simultaneously, undeniably American. It also implies political engagement in issues of importance to Mexican Americans and Mexicans in the United States.)

ROBERTO CLEMENTE

(1934–1972)

BASEBALL PLAYER

Roberto Clemente was the first Latino superstar of Major League Baseball (MLB). He racked up lots of firsts in his eighteen major league seasons—first Latino starting player to help win a World Series in 1960, first Latino to receive a National League Most Valuable Player (MVP) award in 1966, and first Latino to receive a World Series MVP award in 1971. He even racked up a first after his tragic death in 1972; in 1973, he was the first Latino inducted into the Baseball Hall of Fame.

Born in Carolina, Puerto Rico, he was the youngest of seven children. His father was a foreman at a sugarcane plantation, and his mother was a laundress who did additional odd jobs at the plantation. Roberto's father also used his truck to help deliver sand and gravel to the building sites of a construction company. Roberto helped his father load shovels into the construction company's trucks and earned money delivering milk to a nearby store.

Roberto loved baseball and often went to watch games where many Negro League players (and later Major League players) went to play

winter ball. When he was fourteen, Roberto joined a softball team. "I loved the game so much," he wrote in a journal, "that even though our playing field was muddy and we had many trees on it, I used to play many hours every day."

In high school, he excelled at javelin and high jump, and it was thought he might represent Puerto Rico in the Olympics. Later, people would attribute Roberto's strong throwing arm to his training with the javelin, but Roberto saw it differently. "My mother has the same kind of arm, even today at seventy-four," he said in a 1964 interview. "She could throw a ball from second base to home plate with something on it."

"I GOT MY ARM FROM MY MOTHER."

By eighteen, Roberto was playing with the *Cangrejeros de Santurce* (Santurce Crabbers) of the Puerto Rican Baseball League. He caught the eye of a scout for the Brooklyn Dodgers but wasn't signed until 1953. He was looking forward to playing in New York, where he knew many Puerto Ricans lived. But the Dodgers instead sent him to play for their farm team in Montreal, and in the November 1954 draft, the Pittsburgh Pirates—with the worst record in majors during the past season—signed him.

Roberto would play his whole career in the majors with the Pirates. In 1960, his batting average (.312) and ninety-four RBIs led the Pirates to the World Series. Over the next seven years, he won four National League batting titles and an MVP award, and he began what would end up being twelve consecutive Gold Glove award seasons. In 1971, Roberto led the Pirates back to the World Series and was named the MVP of the series. The year after that, he reached his three-thousandth career hit.

Throughout his career, he stood up for himself and other Latino players, who were routinely accused of being lazy and faking injuries. He also worked to get Latino players the recognition he felt they deserved but weren't getting.

Roberto made a point to return to Puerto Rico to hold baseball clinics and play for and then manage Puerto Rican League teams during the winter season. He was there when he heard about the massive earthquake that devastated Managua, Nicaragua's capital city, on December 23, 1972. He raised money and purchased food and medicine to fly into Nicaragua in humanitarian relief. On New Year's Eve, he was on a cargo plane full of supplies headed for Nicaragua when it crashed off the Puerto Rican coast. Everyone on board died, and Roberto's body was never found.

The Baseball Hall of Fame waived its usual five-year waiting period and inducted Roberto after he died. Felipe Alou—the longtime MLB player, coach, and manager—hailed Roberto as "our Jackie Robinson" in acknowledgment of the path he forged for Latino players. Beloved as much for his humanitarian efforts as for his baseball skills, Roberto is an enduring source of pride for Puerto Ricans everywhere.

CELIA CRUZ

(1925–2003)

SINGER

"¡AZÚCAR!"

When Úrsula Hilaria Celia de la Caridad Cruz Alfonso—who would come to be known as Celia Cruz, the "Queen of Salsa"— was born in Havana, Cuba, her grandmother said she was born singing. As a child, Celia sang lullabies for her siblings and cousins, but it wasn't until her mother (who possessed a splendid voice herself) heard Celia sing for a tourist that she knew Celia had a special talent. Celia was twelve years old at the time, and the tourist was so overwhelmed by her singing that he bought her a new pair of shoes. Many tourists and songs later, Celia had secured new shoes for all the children of the neighborhood.

Although Celia's father wanted her to become a teacher, Celia's talent became her calling, and she abandoned her studies just short of becoming certified as a teacher to instead enroll in the National Music Conservatory. She sang on radio programs, usually competing for prizes, and once was paid $15 for her rendition of a tango. In 1950, the director of Cuba's celebrated band *La Sonora Matancera* (which made its name playing the musical form known as *son*) heard her sing and hired her as the lead singer of the group, ushering in what is considered the band's Golden Age. In 1957, Celia picked up her first gold record for her work with Sonora Matancera. And then the Cuban revolution happened.

Fidel Castro, it is said, was a fan of Celia Cruz's singing, but she wasn't a fan of being told what to sing or where to sing it. In 1960, when Sonora Matancera played a concert in Mexico City, Celia decided not to return to Cuba. "I have left everything I love best," she said then, "because I sensed immediately that Fidel Castro wanted to create a communist dictatorship." Her hatred of Castro was sealed in 1962, when her mother died and Celia wasn't permitted to return to Cuba for the burial.

In the United States, she settled down in Fort Lee, New Jersey, with her husband, trumpet player Pedro Knight, to whom she would be married for forty-one years. She quickly established herself and sang with the legendary Tito Puente, Johnny Pacheco, Willie Colón, and the Fania All Stars. She played Carnegie Hall. With her big voice, flamboyant outfits, colorful wigs, infectious energy, and boundless enthusiasm, she became the most renowned face of the salsa scene in the United States and an icon in her own right.

Celia recorded thirty-seven albums during her lifetime, winning three Latin Grammys and two Grammys, one of them a Lifetime Achievement Award. When she died, her casket was flown to Miami so her fans could say good-bye. Two hundred thousand of them showed up for their queen.

OLGA CUSTODIO

(1953—)

MILITARY AND COMMERCIAL AIRLINE PILOT

"I LIKED THE FEELING OF BEING IN THE AIR."

Olga Custodio felt at home in the air. After all, she flew a lot. As the child of a noncommissioned officer and communications specialist in the U.S. Army, she moved with her family from Puerto Rico to Taiwan to New Jersey to Iran to Paraguay, and back again—all before she turned sixteen. She has said she always loved being on airplanes, so is it any surprise she'd want to grow up to fly them?

Olga was born in San Juan, Puerto Rico. She started her education in Taiwan—kindergarten and first grade—and continued her schooling in all those other countries, returning to Puerto Rico when she was fifteen for her last year of high school.

At sixteen, she was accepted into the University of Puerto Rico. She tried to join the ROTC (Reserve Officer Training Corps) at that time, not knowing that women weren't allowed. The recruiter gave her an entrance exam to complete, and Olga turned it in. When she came back several weeks later to see about her score, the recruiter told her she hadn't passed.

She was disappointed, but there was college to attend and new subjects to learn, and it wasn't until much later that she found out she had actually gotten one of the highest scores ever on the test.

After earning her bachelor of arts degree, Olga worked a variety of jobs, got married, and had a child. She was working for the Department of Defense in Panama when she heard that the air force was actively recruiting women to become military pilots. She was mere months away from hitting the age limit (28.5) for cadets to enter pilot training and lived nowhere near an air force recruitment center, but she found an air force tech sergeant willing to help her fill out the recruitment paperwork. When they got to the part where she had to list her top three career choices, she said, "You can write down anything you want on that form, but I'm going to be a pilot, a pilot, or a pilot."

She entered flight screening officer training school in 1980, and after completing the training, she qualified for undergraduate pilot training. A year later, she became the first Latina to complete U.S. Air Force military training.

A second lieutenant, Olga became an instructor at Laughlin Air Force Base in Texas. She became the first woman to be a Northrop T-38 Talon instructor there. When she was later reassigned to Randolph Air Force Base, she became the first female T-38 instructor there, as well.

She was such an accomplished pilot that once, when a bird struck the engine of her T-38 when she was flying in bad weather, she was

able to recover and land the plane. The air force gave her an HQ AETC Aviation Safety Award for her skill.

Olga retired from the Air Force after twenty-three years, with the rank of lieutenant colonel, but she wasn't done flying. She became one of the first Latina commercial airline captains and logged more than eleven thousand flight hours for American Airlines before she retired in 2008.

"What I love best is the view. It's just you, your jet, and the sky," she told an interviewer once. "I had the best office with the best view."

JAIME ESCALANTE

(1930–2010)

EDUCATOR

"I'LL TEACH YOU MATH, AND THAT'S YOUR LANGUAGE."

Born in La Paz, Bolivia, to parents who were both school teachers in an Indigenous Aymara village, Jaime Escalante became one of the best-known teachers in the U.S. and was portrayed by Edward James Olmos in the movie *Stand and Deliver*.

The movie focused on Jaime's 1982 AP Calculus class at Garfield High School in East Los Angeles, where his students—mostly working-class and Latino—scored so well on the AP Calculus exams that they were accused of cheating by the Educational Testing Service. Jaime accused the testing organization of racism. Jaime and his students were vindicated when they performed just as well the second time they were tested.

Jaime taught math and physics for nine years in Bolivia before immigrating to the U.S. in the 1960s. Although he had both his teaching certification and a degree from a university in Bolivia, Jaime worked as a busboy and a cook while he earned his associate degree from Pasadena City College. He worked testing computers as he studied for his bachelor's in mathematics from California State University, Los Angeles.

After he got his teaching certification in 1974, he went to teach at Garfield High School, which was about to lose its accreditation.

His teaching methods were unconventional. Loud music, remote-controlled toys, and magic tricks were all part of it. So was demanding that his students arrive an hour before school and stay several hours after so he could drill them. He instituted Saturday classes and mandatory summer school for them, too. "You're going to go to college and sit in the front row, not in the back," he'd tell his students, "because you are going to know more than anybody."

Jaime met with a lot of resistance from fellow teachers, parents, and even the unions—but his success was undeniable. By 1987, eighty-five of Jaime's students had passed the college-level AP Calculus exam, and many of them went on to universities like MIT and Princeton.

Jaime hosted a Peabody Award–winning instructional show on PBS, *Futures*, which introduced students to math and science careers. In 2016 the U.S. Postal Service issued a commemorative stamp in his honor, acknowledging his contributions to education.

"You have to love the subject you teach," he told NPR in an interview, "and you have to love the kids and make them see that they have a chance, an opportunity in this country to become whatever they want to."

MACARIO GARCÍA

(1920–1972)

STAFF SERGEANT, WORLD WAR II

Macario García was the first Mexican immigrant to receive the U.S. Medal of Honor for heroism in action during World War II. A year later, he received the *Medalla de Mérito Militar*, Mexico's equivalent of the U.S. Medal of Honor. Even though Macario enlisted in the U.S. military in 1942, he wouldn't become a citizen until 1947.

Macario was born in Villa de Castaños, Coahuila, Mexico. His parents were farmworkers, and Macario was one of ten children. In 1923, when he was three, the family immigrated to Sugarland, Texas. Macario picked crops, as did his siblings, and missed many days of school because of the farmwork.

According to the army, Macario enlisted as an infantryman on November 11, 1942, saying that "he felt a strong obligation to give back to the country he had called home for so many years." He was assigned to Bravo Company, First Battalion, Twenty-Second Infantry Regiment, Fourth Infantry Division, and was wounded in action at Normandy in June 1944.

After recovering for four months, he rejoined his unit. In November of that year, in Grosshau, Germany, according to the Medal of Honor citation: "[The] company was pinned down by intense machine-gun fire and subjected to a concentrated artillery and mortar barrage," and Macario was wounded in the shoulder and the foot. He refused to be evacuated then charged two enemy machine-gun nests.

He destroyed the first machine gun with a grenade and, with a rifle, killed three of the enemy soldiers. When he rejoined his company, the second machine gun opened fire. Macario stormed the position, destroyed the machine gun, killed three more enemy soldiers, and cap-

"I'VE BEEN FIGHTING FOR PEOPLE LIKE YOU, AND NOW YOU MISTREAT ME."

tured four. He continued fighting until the company was victorious and only then sought medical attention.

In addition to the Medal of Honor and Mérito Militar, Macario received a Purple Heart, a Bronze Star, and the Combat Infantryman's Badge for his heroic actions. But he remained humble. In an article about receiving the Medal of Honor, which appeared in a local news-paper, Macario explained that his skill with a rifle came from having learned to shoot when he was hunting rabbits and that his greatest desire going forth was to go school and study "scientific farming."

But shortly after he returned to the United States, in 1945, Macario was denied service at a restaurant in Richmond, Texas, because he was

Latino. He and the owner fought (some accounts say that the owner hit Macario with a baseball bat), and the police were called. Macario was arrested and charged in the incident. The case was repeatedly postponed and finally dropped in 1946.

A year later, Macario became a U.S. citizen, and four years later, he earned his high school degree. He would go on to become a counselor with the U.S. Department of Veterans Affairs, and when he died in 1972, he was buried with full military honors.

X GONZÁLEZ

(1999—)

ACTIVIST

‖‖‖‖‖‖‖‖‖‖‖‖‖‖‖‖‖‖‖‖‖‖‖‖‖‖‖‖‖‖‖‖‖‖‖‖‖‖

"WE ARE GOING TO BE THE KIDS YOU READ ABOUT IN TEXTBOOKS."

‖‖‖‖‖‖‖‖‖‖‖‖‖‖‖‖‖‖‖‖‖‖‖‖‖‖‖‖‖‖‖‖‖‖‖‖‖‖

It was their eleven-minute speech in front of the Broward County Courthouse three days after they survived the mass shooting at Marjory Stoneman Douglas High School (MSD) that propelled X González into the limelight. But it was their determination to get gun violence prevention measures enacted that made them into an activist and icon.

X was born in Parkland, Florida, one of three siblings. Their father, a lawyer for a cybersecurity company, immigrated from Cuba; their mother is a math tutor. Shortly after the shooting, X wrote about themself: "I'm eighteen years old, Cuban and bisexual. I'm so indecisive that I can't pick a favorite color, and I'm allergic to twelve things. I draw, paint, crochet, sew, embroider—anything productive I can do with my hands while watching Netflix. But none of this matters anymore."

On the day of the shooting, February 14, 2018, X had been selling valentines during their lunch hour. They were in the auditorium of the school when the fire alarms went off. After an initial attempt to leave, they and the other students from the auditorium were turned back and told to take cover. They were there for two hours, and when they emerged, the world they had known had been irrevocably changed: seventeen of their classmates had been killed.

X appeared on CNN that night, along with their school friend David Hogg, fielding questions from Anderson Cooper. They have said that one of the surprises of the interview was the realization that people were actually listening to what they had to say. Their buzzcut and distinctive personal style quickly made them one of the most recognizable of the survivors and burgeoning student-activists.

Three days after the shooting, when they spoke in front of the Broward Courthouse, X's heartfelt but controlled fury translated into a powerful condemnation of gun violence and the adults who have done little to significantly address it: "The people in the government who were voted into power are lying to us. And us kids seem to be the only ones who notice and are prepared to call B.S. . . . Politicians who sit in their gilded House and Senate seats funded by the N.R.A., telling us nothing could ever be done to prevent this: we call B.S. They say that tougher gun laws do not prevent gun violence: we call B.S."

X was one of the cofounders of the Never Again MSD political action committee and gave another memorable speech at the March for Our Lives protest, which took place on March 24, 2018. Thanks to the activism of X and other MSD survivors, the Florida legislature passed a bill titled the Marjory Stoneman Douglas High School Public Safety Act, which raised the minimum age for buying firearms to twenty-one, instituted waiting periods, required background checks, banned bump stocks, and more.

Because of their activism, X has been subjected to personal verbal attacks and efforts to discredit them, but they continue to advocate for gun control and work to make sure young people's concerns are heard. They believe in their power to effect change and their commitment to be the change. "The world is about to change for the better," X and their friends wrote in an Instagram post after the first March for Our Lives. "This is just the beginning."

LAURIE HERNÁNDEZ

(2000—)

OLYMPIC GYMNAST

▪▪▪▪▪▪▪▪▪▪▪▪▪▪▪▪▪▪▪▪▪▪▪▪▪▪▪▪▪▪▪▪▪▪▪▪▪▪

"I GOT THIS."

▪▪▪▪▪▪▪▪▪▪▪▪▪▪▪▪▪▪▪▪▪▪▪▪▪▪▪▪▪▪▪▪▪▪▪▪▪▪

Balance beams stand four feet, one inch, off the ground. Laurie Hernández stands five feet, one inch. But in August 2016, the gymnast seemed undaunted by the height of what is reportedly the toughest apparatus in the sport of gymnastics. A dazzling routine and a round-off double-pike dismount later, the youngest member of the U.S. women's gymnastics team—sixteen years old at the time—scored high enough to earn a silver medal at the Rio Summer Olympics.

"On beam, I am so comfortable when I am out there so it's just, boop, and it's done," Laurie told one reporter after the win. But "I kind of thought I was going to throw up before I went," she revealed to another.

The New Jersey native of Puerto Rican heritage has been doing

gymnastics since she was five years old, when she grew bored of ballet. As her talents emerged, Laurie's parents were supportive and drove her from classes to meets and back again—whatever was necessary for their daughter's development.

Her career took off in 2012, when she qualified for the National Championships in St. Louis. In 2013, she was added to the U.S. Junior National Team, but injuries kept her out of competition in 2014. After competing throughout 2015, Laurie was named to the U.S. Senior National Team in 2016 and then named to the Olympic team.

The rest, as they say, is history.

The Final Five, as the team called itself, won the team gold medal, and Laurie went on to win the individual silver, making her a personal hero to many Latinxs. She is proud of her heritage. "I think it's amazing that I can just go out there and be myself, and the fact that I'm carrying Puerto Rico on my back a little bit, I think that's an honor," she has said.

After her Olympic success, Laurie took time off to write a book for adults (*I Got This: To Gold and Beyond*) and a children's book (*She's Got This*), won a *Dancing with the Stars* competition, and cohosted *American Ninja Warrior Junior*.

JUAN FELIPE HERRERA

(1948—)

U.S. POET LAUREATE

The son of Mexican immigrant farmworkers in California, Juan Felipe Herrera held the highest post any U.S. poet can aspire to—U.S. Poet Laureate. He was the first Latino to be appointed to the Library of Congress position, which requires the poet to undertake a public project to broaden the audience for poetry.

While serving from 2015 to 2017, he said, "I want to assist with closing the gap of knowing about and hearing about our Latino communities in terms of literature, in terms of writing. . . . And I want our young Latinos and Latinas to write their hearts out and express their hearts out and let us all listen to each other."

"I WANT TO WRITE ABOUT HOPE."

JUAN FELIPE HERRERA

For his project, *La Casa de Colores* (*The House of Colors*), Juan Felipe undertook two tasks keyed to the idea of a collective home. The first, under the title *El Jardín* (*The Garden*), was an effort to point people to the beauty and bounty represented by the people's library, the Library of Congress. The other task, under the title *La Familia* (*The Family*), was an epic poem about the American experience that he, along with everyday Americans, would write.

"Yes, I am the first Latino poet laureate in the United States. But I'm also here for everyone and from everyone. My voice is made by everyone's voices."

He grew up speaking Spanish at home, but in school, Juan Felipe was shamed into not speaking it. He graduated from high school in San Diego in 1967 and then attended UCLA on scholarship. He was already writing poetry. In fact, he was writing poetry instead of the traditional term papers required by his university classes. (He got an A- on a forty-page poem he turned in for an economics class).

He went on to get master's degrees at Stanford and at the University of Iowa and held faculty positions first at California State University, Los Angeles, and later at the University of California, Riverside, and then as a visiting professor at the University of Michigan. He published many books of poetry while he taught at those universities, and he involved himself in community building and Chicano civil rights.

Juan Felipe says that, as he listened carefully to people during his time as poet laureate, he heard that many were in pain and experiencing unfairness in this country. While at first these stories made him angry, he eventually realized that underpinning them was a sense of hope and promise for what could be.

DOLORES HUERTA

(1930—)

LABOR ORGANIZER, CIVIL RIGHTS ACTIVIST

When President Barack Obama presented Dolores Huerta with the Presidential Medal of Freedom in 2012, he described the starting point of her legacy of advocacy: "When César Chávez sat Dolores Huerta down at his kitchen table and told her they should start a union, she thought he was joking. She was a single mother of seven children, so she obviously didn't have a lot of free time. But Dolores had been an elementary school teacher and remembered seeing children come to school hungry and without shoes. So, in the end, she agreed—and workers everywhere are glad that she did."

As cofounder of the National Farm Workers Association, which later became the United Farm Workers (UFW), Dolores worked on the Delano grape strike in 1965, along with Chávez. A photo of the young Dolores holding up a *"Huelga"* ("Strike") sign has become symbolic of the many fights she and Chávez led advocating for farmworkers' right to unionize. (See the entry for César Chávez for more about his work.)

Born in New Mexico, she was the second of three children. Her father—a farmer and miner who went on to become a legislator in New Mexico—and mother divorced when Dolores was three years old. Dolores credits her mother—who worked as a waitress and cannery worker until she could buy a small hotel and restaurant in Stockton, California—with instilling in her both her sense of social justice and her feminism.

Dolores was smart, and she experienced racism during her school years from those who did not expect Mexican American students to excel. She earned an associate teaching degree from the University of

"SÍ, SE PUEDE." (YES, WE CAN.)

the Pacific's Delta College and taught for a few years before deciding she could do more good for her students by advocating for, and organizing, their farmworker parents.

Her talent, she has said, was for lobbying and negotiating. She is credited with developing some of the key strategies of the UFW and was critical in securing Aid for Dependent Families and disability insurance for farmworkers in 1963. Her efforts ensured the passage of the Agricultural Labor Relations Act of 1975, which granted farmworkers in California the right to collectively organize and bargain for better wages and working conditions. Robert F. Kennedy acknowledged her help when he won the 1968 California Democratic presidential primary just moments before he was assassinated in Los Angeles.

In 1988, at the age of fifty-eight, Dolores was brutally beaten by police in San Francisco, where she was protesting the use of pesticides in growing table grapes. She had a long recovery from her life-threatening injuries. The incident, which was caught on videotape, helped push the San Francisco Police Department into instituting changes, but it didn't change Dolores's commitment to activism.

She has remained a dedicated activist—and beloved and respected Latina icon—through the years. In 2014, she had the Dolores Huerta Foundation set up a nonprofit, Border Kids' Relief Project, to address the needs of unaccompanied minors at the southern U.S. border. "We are talking about children who need our protection, our assistance, our love," she said then.

In 2016, Dolores worked with People for the American Way, seeking to encourage Latino voter registration and participation. Her foundation continues to provide training and resources related to community organizing to rural, low-income communities and gives them a platform to advocate for change.

Even at eighty-nine years old, Dolores has retained her reputation for fierceness. She was arrested in 2019 at a meeting of the Fresno County (California) Board of Supervisors, where she was protesting the low pay of home health workers. "All of these supervisors make over $100,000 a year, while these people have gone without a wage increase for eleven years, and it's time. *Que es tiempo*," she said. "If supervisors can't take the heat, they should get out of the kitchen."

ÓSCAR DE LA RENTA

(1932–2014)

FASHION DESIGNER

He wanted to be a painter, but he fell into fashion design by chance, and by the end of his life, he had created designs that made him the favorite of three U.S. First Ladies (Jackie Kennedy, Nancy Reagan, and Hillary Clinton) and countless stars such as Nicole Kidman, Kristen Stewart, Penelope Cruz, Oprah Winfrey, and Amal Clooney.

Born in 1932 in Santo Domingo, Dominican Republic, Óscar Aristedes de la Renta was the son of a Dominican mother and Puerto Rican father, the youngest of seven siblings, and the only boy—a fact that, he said, helped him get his way most of the time.

His father wanted Óscar to join his insurance business when he graduated from high school in Santo Domingo, but Óscar decided to go to Spain to study painting at the Royal Academy of Fine Arts of San Fernando instead. There, he fell in love with the culture and vibe of Madrid and spent more time frequenting flamenco venues and cafés than taking classes. His extravagances were paid for by a monthly stipend he received from his father and by his own enterprising nature:

Óscar leveraged his fine arts training to sell fashion sketches to the local newspapers.

He'd later remember those sketches as neither very original nor very good, but they caught the eye of Francesca Lodge, the wife of John Davis Lodge, the American ambassador to Spain, and she asked him to design a gown for her daughter's debutante ball. Both the debutante and the gown Óscar had designed for her appeared on the cover of *Life*—in those days an influential and widely read U.S. magazine—and Óscar's career was born.

"NEVER, EVER CONFUSE WHAT HAPPENS ON A RUNWAY WITH FASHION. A RUNWAY IS SPECTACLE. IT'S ONLY FASHION WHEN A WOMAN PUTS IT ON."

He was hired to sketch dresses for clients at the salon of famed couturier Cristóbal Balenciaga, and later at the Lanvin fashion house, where Spanish movie-costume designer Antonio Castillo called the shots. Castillo asked Óscar if he knew how to cut, drape, and sew before he hired him. Óscar had only sketched and designed on paper, but said he could, and then managed to convince the owner of a local fashion school to condense two years of lessons into the two weeks he had before starting work at Lanvin.

Two years later, in 1963, Óscar moved to New York to design for Elizabeth Arden and, soon after that, established his own brand and went on to international renown. Óscar became an American citizen in 1971, but he never forgot where he came from. He organized benefit fashion shows and financed projects offering assistance to women and children in need in the Dominican Republic. He founded and sustained *El Hogar del Niño*, where 1,200 low-income children were housed and fed and received health care and education. After his first wife died, he adopted a child from *El Hogar del Niño*. His son, Moises, would go on to follow in his father's footsteps—first studying painting, then becoming a fashion designer.

Óscar married for a second time, and with his wife, son, and step-children, he divided his time between his home in Connecticut, a house in Punta Cana, and a farm in La Romana in the Dominican Republic.

In 1993, Óscar would become the first designer from the Americas to be asked to design for the storied French fashion house of Pierre Balmain, but neither that accomplishment nor any other during his long career meant as much to him as family: "After the applause, I have (and have always had) the warmth of family and friends, who are the center of my life."

JENNIFER LOPEZ

(1969—)

ACTRESS, SINGER

Getting ready to go on her latest worldwide tour, Jennifer Lopez hasn't forgotten her roots. Born to Puerto Rican parents Guadalupe and David Lopez, Jennifer grew up in the Bronx, the northernmost borough in New York City. With its significant African American and Latino neighborhoods and its history of working-class pride, the Bronx has nurtured a wide range of dance and music—including a strong influence on hip-hop—and counts some stellar Latinas as native daughters: Jennifer, Supreme Court Justice Sonia Sotomayor, and Congresswoman Alexandria Ocasio-Cortez.

Taking singing and dancing lessons at the age of five, Jennifer would often perform with her sisters, and her love and affection for the performing arts stuck with her as she grew. Despite her parents' wishes for her to get a more conventional job, Jennifer would not abandon her dream. She started acting in small television roles and auditioned and performed as a backup dancer for big names like New Kids on the Block and Janet Jackson.

Then came her big break: *Selena.*

Playing the film role of Tejana singer Selena Quintanilla, Jennifer Lopez was thrust into the spotlight, right where she wanted to be. Awards and commendations of her performance came pouring in, and suddenly she was a household name.

Jennifer has sold over eighty million records and starred in more than a hundred movies and television shows. A superstar and celebrity, Jennifer is arguably the most influential Latina in the United States, and sometimes that has weighed heavily on her—as when her personal life has come under scrutiny. But it has also enabled her to make a real impact through her philanthropy.

"I'M STILL JENNY FROM THE BLOCK."

Closest to her heart is the Lopez Family Foundation (LFF), a non-profit she cofounded with her sister Lynda. The goal of LFF is to increase the accessibility of health care for women and children. In addition, Jennifer has spoken up about the #MeToo movement, sharing her own experiences to support and lift up others affected, and she has participated in petitioning the U.S. Congress to enact gun control after the deadly 2016 shooting at Pulse nightclub in Orlando.

Jennifer may not live in the Bronx anymore, but she has never forgotten what it's given her: the power to believe, the power to persevere, and the power to succeed.

XIUHTEZCATL MARTÍNEZ

(2000—)

INDIGENOUS CLIMATE ACTIVIST

When Xiuhtezcatl Martínez was six years old, he addressed a crowd of three hundred people about climate change. At age nine, he convinced the city council in Boulder, Colorado, to ban the use of chemical pesticides in the city parks. By sixteen, he had already addressed the United Nations (UN) five times. For Xiuhtezcatl, it is all part of fighting for the Earth and for future generations—something he doesn't think previous generations have done well or, really, at all.

"My generation is not going to sit idly by while they bicker and argue and fail to do their job as leaders, because in all honesty, we, the youth of the planet, we are the leaders," Xiuhtezcatl has said. "If you look at the movement about climate change now, it's being led by youth."

Born in Boulder, Colorado, Xiuhtezcatl and his younger brother and sister were raised by their Indigenous Mexica father, Siri Martínez, and non-Indigenous mother, Tamara Roske, to be caretakers of the planet.

Tamara is director of the Earth Guardians, a worldwide environmental and climate justice organization she founded in Hawaii, for which Xiuhtezcatl serves as youth director.

Xiuhtezcatl has said he started learning traditional Mexica dances as soon as he could walk and learned to speak Nahuatl as soon as he could talk. He is trilingual and has, on occasion, preceded a UN address in English with prayers in Spanish and Nahuatl. Mexica Indigenous traditions also prompt him to protect the things that make the world

"WE ARE STANDING HERE TO FIGHT AND PROTECT EVERYTHING THAT WE LOVE."

sacred, which means taking action.

In addition to delivering an impassioned TED talk and releasing a hip-hop anti-fracking song and video, he is best known as one of the lead plaintiffs in a youth-led lawsuit against the U.S. government arguing that by ignoring climate change, the federal government has jeopardized their continued existence and future.

"I stand before you representing my entire generation," he said as he addressed the UN when he was fifteen years old. "Youth are standing up all over the planet to find solutions. We are flooding the streets and now flooding the courts. We need you to take action. We are all indigenous to this earth.".

SYLVIA MÉNDEZ

(1936—)

CIVIL RIGHTS ACTIVIST

The year was 1943. Sylvia Méndez had just turned eight and was attending Hoover Elementary School in Westminster, California, with her brothers Gonzalo Jr. and Jerome. But Sylvia's parents were hardly pleased about that: Hoover Elementary was a small, run-down building meant to segregate Latino children from white children. Unhappy with the quality of education, the lack of funding, and the discrimination his family faced, Gonzalo Méndez sent Sylvia and her brothers with their Aunt Sally to enroll in the all-white school, Seventeenth Street Elementary.

Despite their desire to learn, the Méndez children were denied enrollment based on the color of their skin. Enraged, Gonzalo and his wife, Felicitas, took to the courts, filing a lawsuit against the education board of Orange County; they fought against the segregation and racism that prevented their children—and five thousand other Latino children—from receiving better education and equal opportunities. Though the legal process was long and often frustrating, the Méndez

family received the support of other civil rights groups, such as the NAACP, the ACLU, and more.

Finally, in 1947, the landmark court case *Mendez v. Westminster* was over, and public schools and spaces in California were to be desegregated. Sylvia and her brothers were finally allowed admittance into Seventeenth Street Elementary, though it did little to alleviate the racism and prejudice both the students and staff expressed against Latino students.

"I TOLD MY MOTHER I CAN'T [KEEP FIGHTING DISCRIMINATION], I'M A NURSE, AND SHE TOLD ME, 'SYLVIA, SOMEONE HAS TO DO IT.'"

Despite this, Sylvia would go on to attend and graduate from college, working as a nurse for over thirty years until her mother's health started to decline. When Gonzalo died in 1964, he had been unaware of the impact *Mendez v. Westminster* had on Thurgood Marshall, the attorney who had taken *Brown v. Board of Education* to the U.S. Supreme Court in 1954. Upset by the glossing over of their lawsuit in the history of desegregation, Felicitas urged her daughter to continue the fight to end discrimination against Latinos.

SYLVIA MÉNDEZ

Sylvia has worked to fight against segregation, speaking at universities and in front of legislators. In 2011, she was awarded the Presidential Medal of Freedom by President Barack Obama for her continued activism.

A Latina of both Mexican and Puerto Rican heritage, Sylvia continues to speak out against discrimination, encouraging both parents and students to overcome "the impossible so that their children finish their studies because this is what will allow them to progress."

LIN-MANUEL MIRANDA

(1980—)

ACTOR, PLAYWRIGHT, COMPOSER

He's a household name now. His creations are plastered across billboards and have topped the charts for weeks on end, with tickets sold out for months in advance. His quote "love is love is love" appears in placards and banners in LGBT Pride celebrations throughout the nation.

Lin-Manuel Miranda has become one of the most well-known contemporary composers, and it's thanks to the artist's improbable vision that the story of the first U.S. secretary of the treasury—Alexander Hamilton—deserved a hip-hop musical performed by a cast comprised, in its majority, of actors of color. His casting choices were in answer to Broadway's lack of diversity and inclusion and were meant to advance equity in casting and roles.

Born in 1980 to Luz and Luis Miranda, Lin-Manuel has always had a talent for music; when he was young, he would write fun little jingles.

While attending Wesleyan University, he wrote a draft of what would become the Tony Award–winning musical *In the Heights*, set in the predominantly Dominican neighborhood of Washington Heights in New York City. In 2008, he began his journey into becoming Hamilton.

When Lin-Manual performed at the White House Evening of Poetry, Music, and the Spoken Word, it was his first foray into uncovering who the Caribbean-immigrant founding father Alexander Hamilton really was. He would continue to study and draft and expand his piece until 2015, when *Hamilton* was completed. And boy, did the world react. The

"LOVE IS LOVE IS LOVE."

musical was so successful, so well-loved, it won sixteen Tony Awards and captivated the United States and much of the world.

But Lin-Manuel didn't just stop after *Hamilton*—he's composed the music for major motion pictures and live-stage adaptations of classic movies. He has been recognized for his creativity and talent with several Emmys, Grammys, and Pulitzers, as well as Kennedy Center Honors and a MacArthur Genius Fellowship.

He is, perhaps, most respected for his humanitarian work. Following the devastating hurricanes Irma and María in 2017, Lin-Manuel focused his energies on helping Puerto Rico rebuild from the catastrophe. He wrote and released a benefit Puerto Rican all-star song, "Almost Like Praying," and scheduled a limited run of *Hamilton* to be performed on the island—with most of the proceeds being funneled into the reconstruction efforts. He has been outspoken about debt forgiveness for the island—which as a commonwealth isn't afforded the same protections from bankruptcy as states—and continues to raise awareness of Puerto Rico's situation, urging his fans to make a difference, to be better.

With frequent discussions and fundraisers and articles shared on his Twitter account, Lin-Manuel is a force of positivity and inspiration for Puerto Rico and for the rest of the nation.

C. DAVID MOLINA

(1926–1996)

EMERGENCY ROOM PHYSICIAN, FOUNDER OF MOLINA HEALTHCARE, INC.

IIIIIIIIIIIIIIIIIIIIIIIIIIIIIIIIIIIIIIIIIIIIIIIIIIII

"WHEN YOU HELP IT IS NOT TO GET OTHERS PEOPLE'S ATTENTION OR TO RECEIVE GLORY, IT IS BECAUSE IT IS THE RIGHT THING TO DO."

IIIIIIIIIIIIIIIIIIIIIIIIIIIIIIIIIIIIIIIIIIIIIIIIIIII

C. David Molina is considered a pioneer in managed health care, but he didn't start out with an interest in public health or even medicine. He was going to be a teacher.

Born and raised in Yuma, Arizona, David studied education at San Diego State College. He taught elementary school in Yuma and in Long

Beach before deciding to get his medical degree from the California College of Medicine (now University of California, Irvine). He would later get a master's degree in public health from UCLA.

As a physician, David established Long Beach's first intensive care unit at Pacific Hospital and was the director of the hospital's emergency department for twenty-one years. He also developed the city's paramedic system and trained the first teams of firefighters with EMT training. In his work at Pacific Hospital, he noticed that low-income, uninsured, and non–English-speaking people were going to the emergency room in need of nonemergency health care.

He wondered how he could best serve those patients, who were very often Latinos. In 1985, he opened a clinic in the back of a doctor's office in Long Beach as a way to provide regular medical care for those without access. This was the start of Molina Healthcare. It was a family enterprise. His wife and their five children became involved in the organization as it expanded to two more locations. After the medical center was awarded a state contract, it grew exponentially: there were 12 offices and 10,000 members of what had become a health management organization.

By the time of David's death in 1996, Molina Healthcare had 105,000 members, 29 offices, and 8,000 additional health service providers in its network. In 2003, the company had grown to 500,000 members and was a publicly traded company on the New York Stock Exchange; by 2015, it had 3.5 million members, serving people in multiple states.

His legacy of giving back to the community remains through the Fortune 500 company he founded, his children and the work they continue to do for others, and the Smithsonian Latino Center's Molina Family Latino Gallery, the first dedicated space to tell Latino stories at the nation's museum.

RITA MORENO

(1931—)

ACTOR, SINGER, DANCER

Rita Moreno is the only Latina, and one of the few performers of any ethnicity, to have won an Emmy, a Grammy, an Oscar, and a Tony (the esteemed EGOT). Add to that her Presidential Medal of Freedom, her National Medal of the Arts, and her Kennedy Center Lifetime Artistic Achievement Award, and you begin to get a sense of how talented and accomplished this seventy-year veteran of the entertainment industry really is.

She was born in Humacao, Puerto Rico, in 1931, but her mother brought her to New York City when she was four years old. They lived in a tenement apartment and, according to Rita, were very poor. "My greatest longing was to be in show business and my mom allowed me to pursue it. Like many [migrant] mothers, she spent much of her life just getting by—all the while encouraging me to pursue my dreams."

Rita made it to Hollywood by the age of seventeen but encountered deep racism that would persist even after she had played one of

her most notable roles—Anita in the film *West Side Story*—for which she won the Best Supporting Actress Oscar in 1962. "I was always offered the stereotypical Latina roles," she said in 2008. "The Conchitas and Lolitas in westerns. I was always barefoot. It was humiliating, embarrassing stuff. But I did it because there was nothing else. After *West Side Story*, it was pretty much the same thing. A lot of gang stories."

She did a lot of TV work, including children's shows, where her warmth and personality shone through. Fittingly, her 1972 Grammy is

"IT IS THROUGH ART THAT WE WILL PREVAIL AND WE WILL ENDURE. IT LIVES ON AFTER US AND DEFINES US AS PEOPLE."

for Best Album for Children and celebrates the work she did with *The Electric Company*, the Emmy-winning TV series from Children's Television Workshop (now Sesame Workshop).

Rita won a Tony in 1975 for Best Featured Actress in a play for her work in *The Ritz*; her first Emmy in 1977, for Individual Performance in a Variety or Music Program; and a second Emmy in 1978 for Outstanding Guest Actress in a Drama Series for her work on *The Rockford Files*.

She has always been civically engaged. She participated in the March on Washington in 1963 and today encourages young people and Latinos to register to vote and participate in our democracy.

At eighty-seven, Rita is quick to remind others what it takes to realize your dreams. "Persevere," she says. "Don't let anybody tell you what is good for you. Don't let anyone spoil your vision of what your life should be. You know best, and you will persevere."

ELLEN OCHOA

(1958—)

ENGINEER, ASTRONAUT

Ellen Ochoa was the first Latina in space. In 1993, she spent nine days aboard the space shuttle *Discovery* as a mission specialist. Her charge was to gather information about damage to the Earth's ozone layer. It wouldn't be the last time Ellen would be in space. During her four flights, she logged more than one thousand hours in space.

Ellen was born in Los Angeles and grew up in La Mesa, California. She showed an early aptitude for math and science and graduated at the top of her class from San Diego State University, with a bachelor's degree in physics. She wasn't sure whether she wanted to be a concert flutist or an engineer, but she finally opted for the latter, earning her master's and doctorate from Stanford University in electrical engineering.

While she was pursuing her doctorate, she followed the career of Sally Ride, the first woman astronaut, with interest. This prompted Ellen to go into the aerospace industry after she completed her degree, first working at the optics lab at Sandia National Laboratories in New Mexico. Ellen developed three patented optical devices while she was there.

After moving back to California, she helped develop optical and computer systems for automated space exploration for NASA. In 1990, she applied for entry to NASA's highly competitive astronaut training program and was accepted.

She says she never felt any sort of hesitation from NASA about her being a Latina. "I've had wonderful opportunities at NASA. I really feel like I've been encouraged all the way along. I think there was a time before I joined, when women and minorities first joined, where there was a little bit of 'how is this going to work?' But by the time I was in office, people just really wanted to see if you were going to be a good team member or not, if you know your stuff, and if you are doing everything to get the job done."

In 2013, Ellen became the second woman and first Latina director of NASA's Johnson Space Center. Through 2018, she oversaw the astronauts, the Orion program, and mission operations for the International Space Station.

"WHAT EVERYONE IN THE ASTRONAUT CORPS SHARES IN COMMON IS NOT GENDER OR ETHNIC BACKGROUND, BUT MOTIVATION, PERSEVERANCE, AND DESIRE... TO PARTICIPATE IN A VOYAGE OF DISCOVERY."

JORGE RAMOS

(1958—)

NEWS ANCHOR, AUTHOR

||||||||||||||||||||||||||||||||||||||||||

"I HAVE THE RIGHT TO ASK A QUESTION."

||||||||||||||||||||||||||||||||||||||||||

He is one of the most watched news anchors in the United States and yet is so unfamiliar to most Anglos that they can pass him on the street without doing a celebrity double take. He is Jorge Ramos, Univision's longtime anchor and a Mexican-born U.S. citizen and immigrant advocate. Millions of Spanish-speaking Latinos tune in to watch his nightly newscast, and in 2016, when he started streaming content live from Facebook, millions watched him there, as well.

The dapper, white-haired journalist studied communications in Mexico and worked first in radio before moving on to TV, where his employer was Mexico's largest media conglomerate. In 1983, he quit

Televisa after a story he produced that was critical of Mexico's government was censored. He sold his personal belongings and came to the United States on a student visa.

His first journalism job in the United States was at KMEX (Channel 34), a Spanish-language TV station in Los Angeles, which later became Univision. He met his longtime Univision coanchor María Elena Salinas at KMEX. His big break at Univision came after he was transferred to the Miami headquarters. "Miami has been incredibly generous to Latinos," he said in 2015. "As one of my first bosses here told me, 'It's the only city in America where we're not treated as second-class citizens.'"

In 2008, Jorge became a citizen of the United States, and he has said that his citizenship gives him the right to ask politicians tough questions about their policies and rhetoric. In 2015, when then-presidential candidate Donald Trump told him to sit down at a press conference in which Jorge was peppering him with questions about his immigration plans, Jorge refused and kept asking his questions. "I knew it was right not to sit down. If I had sat down, Latinos would have been so disappointed." That same year, *Time* magazine selected Jorge as one of the world's hundred most influential people.

Jorge coanchored the Univision news desk with María Elena Salinas for more than three decades until she stepped down from the role in 2017. He has swum across the Rio Grande in pursuit of a story, challenged presidents, won eight Emmys, authored thirteen books, and never shied away from the rigors of his job. There may be no other Spanish-speaking person in the United States whom Latinos trust more.

SYLVIA RIVERA

(1951–2002)

TRANSGENDER ACTIVIST

Sylvia Rivera was three years old when her mother died, three years after her father left them. It was the year 1954, and she had been sent to live with her *abuelita* (grandmother). But things were not so happy in that house, and at age eleven, Sylvia ran away for good after her grandmother disapproved of her wearing makeup and dressing like a girl. By the time she had turned nineteen, Rivera had reinvented herself as an outspoken young woman, working to combat discrimination and racism among the LGBT community. She joined the Gay Activists Alliance, which sought to gain the fundamental, inalienable rights that had been denied to them.

Though some dispute her involvement in the Stonewall Riots, Sylvia was a close friend of the movement's founding figure, Marsha P. Johnson. Many LGBT rights historians have included her in their recounting of the Stonewall Riots in part because of her racial identity: of both Puerto Rican and Venezuelan descent, Sylvia Rivera represents the often overlooked population of LGBT and queer Latinx. Indeed, she

often fought to defend and represent those she felt were marginalized and outcast within the LGBT community. She and Johnson founded Street Transvestite Action Revolutionaries (STAR), which sought to gain civil rights for LGBT and queer individuals.

Up until her death in 2002, Sylvia continued to fight for equality within the LGBT community, giving impassioned speeches and working within the groups she helped found as well as with others. She worked

"I AM TIRED OF SEEING MY CHILDREN...YOU ARE ALL MY CHILDREN...I AM TIRED OF SEEING HOMELESS TRANSGENDER CHILDREN."

closely with groups like the Human Rights Campaign and participated in discussions and debates over political policies like "Don't Ask, Don't Tell" in the U.S. military and the marriage equality movement. Sylvia's legacy continues to inspire Latinx members of the queer community, influencing and motivating the future leaders of the civil rights move- ment. In an interview she gave before her death, Sylvia said, "I'm not missing a minute of this. It's the revolution!" So be inspired by Sylvia's determination and her integrity: fight for what you believe in; don't stand to the side.

MARÍA ELENA SALINAS

(1954—)

NEWS ANCHOR

Like labor organizers Dolores Huerta and César Chávez, who are frequently mentioned in the same breath, it is difficult to mention María Elena Salinas without picturing her at the Univision anchor desk in the company of her coanchor of three decades, Jorge Ramos. The image persists even now that she's stepped down from her anchor post and become a contributor to CBS News. But María Elena's achievements are her own.

She was born in Los Angeles to Mexican parents who had immigrated to the United States in the 1940s. After María Elena's birth, the family moved back to Mexico until she was eight, then returned to live in the United States. "My mother taught us to love the country where we were born and the country of our heritage. So we celebrated and embraced both cultures and holidays, like the Fourth of July and Mexican Independence Day, Thanksgiving and Las Posadas. That's why I feel I'm part of that generation of bilingual-bicultural Hispanics in the U.S., who are very proud of their roots."

When María Elena was fourteen, she started working so she could help her parents pay the rent. For many Latinos, family is life's hub, and it is not unusual for Latino teens, if the family is struggling financially, to juggle school and jobs that help pay the bills. After high school, María Elena went to a community college in Los Angeles for two years and studied marketing. She wouldn't study broadcast journalism until she had already started working, and then she'd do it via extension courses from UCLA.

María Elena worked at a radio station, and then in 1981, moved onto television, working at the Spanish-language KMEX (Channel 34) in Los

"I'M NOT AN IMPORT FROM LATIN AMERICA. I'M HOMEGROWN."

Angeles. The station was so small that she was doing reporting, serving as an anchor, and doing public service and entertainment programs. The station was owned by Spanish International Network (which would later become Univision and have its national headquarters in Miami). At one point, half the national staff left (to form what would become Univision's main competition, Telemundo), and María Elena ended up anchoring the national late-night news program.

In 1988, a new news director teamed María Elena, who had been anchoring the eleven p.m. news, and Jorge Ramos, who had been anchoring the six thirty p.m. news, and made them coanchors of the primetime news program. They would serve together for decades and become the most trusted voices in Spanish-language media in the United States.

María Elena has interviewed everyone from President Barack Obama to the rebel leader of the Zapatistas in Mexico, and during the course of her career, she has won Emmys, the Edward R. Murrow Award, and Peabody Awards for her broadcast journalism. The Univision newscast she coanchored has grown and now routinely beats the three English-language national network newscasts (ABC, CBS, NBC) in the ratings war in the Los Angeles and Miami markets.

"I remember people telling me when I started working at KMEX, 'You really should try to make a transition into English TV, because there's no future in Spanish-language TV, because Latinos will assimilate,'" she has said. "And look what has happened now. Not only is the Hispanic community the fastest-growing community, but Spanish-language media is the fastest-growing media, and our viewership continues to grow."

María Elena believes in the need for and the power of Spanish-language media in the United States—so much so that she has created a scholarship at the National Association of Hispanic Journalists for young journalists who want to pursue careers in U.S. Spanish-language media. She is also very clear that she wants to correct the notion that U.S. Latinos are somehow "less American" than other citizens.

"I'm proud of who I am and what my community has accomplished," she says.

SONIA SOTOMAYOR

(1954—)

ASSOCIATE JUSTICE, U.S. SUPREME COURT

"THE LATINA IN ME IS AN EMBER THAT BLAZES FOREVER."

She was President Barack Obama's first choice for the job.

She is a Princeton graduate, a Yale graduate, and has over thirty years' experience in law and jurisprudence. She is also the first Latina Supreme Court justice.

Her name is Sonia Sotomayor.

Born in the Bronx in 1954 to Puerto Ricans born on the island, Sonia was especially close to her grandmother. She gave Sonia a sense of direction, inspiring her to be firm in her convictions and stand up for what she believes. And it was that determination that set Sonia on the path to the Supreme Court. Growing up with type 1 diabetes, Sonia learned how to manage and regulate her daily insulin shots; her diabetes ultimately kept her from her childhood dream of being a detective like Nancy Drew, but it didn't stop her from dreaming big. By the age of ten, Sonia had decided she wanted to be an attorney.

In order to pursue her (second) childhood dream, Sonia would have to get a world-class education. So she studied hard, worked hard, and ended up at Princeton University. Upset with the lack of Latina professors and Latin American courses while she was there, she fought to improve the diversity of the school's faculty. She petitioned the school board, eventually seeing her efforts reflected in Princeton's hiring of more Latino faculty. After leaving Princeton with a bachelor's degree, Sonia moved on to Yale University and the bar exam. And just like that, she was a lawyer.

She started working as an assistant district attorney for New York City in 1979, becoming heavily involved in all types of litigation—shoplifting, robberies, murder. She was as fearless then as she is now.

It wasn't until 1991 that she became a judge, but she set the record: the youngest judge for the Southern District of New York City and the first Latina federal judge in the whole state.

She had an extensive résumé of court cases, ranging from business and education reform to civil rights cases and property rights. And it was her tenacity that led President Obama to nominate her to the Supreme Court. In 2009, she became the first Latina associate justice on the court.

She rules on important national issues: in 2012, she ruled on the *Arizona v. United States* case, which centered on the constitutionality of Arizona SB 1070, which, at the time, was the harshest anti-illegal immigration measure in the nation. Nicknamed the Show Me Your Papers law, it called for fining (and even jailing) law enforcement who refused to help identify undocumented immigrants. Sonia and four other justices ruled against the bill, able to strike down the more appalling components and reach a compromise with the law's writers.

In addition to her prowess as a Supreme Court justice, Sonia has kept close ties to her Puerto Rican heritage, visiting the island frequently and participating in discussions of Puerto Rican statehood. She is also concerned with literacy, and in addition to writing two children's books (*Just Ask!: Be Different, Be Brave, Be You* and *Turning the Pages: My Life Story*), she's made notable appearances on *Sesame Street*.

"Experience has taught me that you cannot value dreams according to the odds of their coming true. Their real value is in stirring within us the will to aspire."

DARA TORRES

(1967—)

OLYMPIC SWIMMER, SPORTS COMMENTATOR, AUTHOR

"WHY CAN'T A 41-YEAR-OLD MOM TRY FOR AN OLYMPIC TEAM?"

Dara Torres has won twelve Olympic medals. In 1984, she was the first swimmer to represent the United States in Olympic competition, and in 2008, she was the oldest. She brought home three silver medals at the age of forty-one, turning the Cuban American swimmer into an icon for older athletes.

She was born in Los Angeles and started swimming when she was seven. She joined her school team and swam on it until her junior year of high school, when she started training for her first Olympics. During the 1984 Olympics in Los Angeles, she was on the freestyle relay team, which won a team gold.

Dara went on to attend the University of Florida in Gainesville on an athletic scholarship, and there she participated in National Collegiate

Athletic Association (NCAA) competitions and won twenty-eight All American swimming honors. At the 1988 Olympics in Seoul, South Korea, she earned a bronze medal as part of the freestyle relay team and a silver medal as part of the medley relay team. At the 1992 Olympics in Barcelona, she again earned a gold medal as part of the freestyle relay team.

Dara then took a seven-year break from competitive swimming. When she was thirty-two and the Olympics in Sydney, Australia, were a year away, she started training again. She wound up winning five medals in Sydney—two team golds and three individual bronzes.

At the 2000 Olympic games, Dara was the oldest member of the swim team at age thirty-three; at the 2008 Olympics in Beijing, she was, at forty-one, the oldest U.S. Olympic swimmer in history and the first to compete in five Olympic games. She won three silver medals. "When I decided to make this comeback, there were two kinds of people I encountered when I was doing this. There was the type that asked, 'Aren't you too old?' and then the other type that told me, 'If anyone can do it, you can do it.' And I started to think about it: you have [golfer] Jack Nicklaus who can win a Masters at 46 years old or you have Nolan Ryan who can pitch a no-hitter at 44 years old. Why can't a 41-year-old mom try for an Olympic team?"

At forty-five, she just missed qualifying to compete at the 2012 London Olympics and decided then to retire from competitive swimming. After her career as an Olympian was over, Dara became a sports commentator, working with ESPN, CNN, and Fox, among others. She has written two best-selling books: *Age Is Just a Number: Achieve Your Dreams at Any Stage in Your Life* (2009) and *Gold Medal Fitness: A Revolutionary 5-Week Program* (2010).

ROBERT UNANUE

(circa 1966—)

CEO

You may not have heard the name Robert Unanue, but chances are you've seen his business's products at your grocery store: canned black beans, boxes of Spanish-style rice, olive oil, saffron spice mixes, guava juice, and coconut water. Robert—more often called Bob—runs Goya Foods, the largest Latino-owned family food company in the United States.

Bob's great-grandfather Prudencio Unanue Ortiz immigrated from Spain to Puerto Rico, where he established a small food distribution business. In 1918, he went to New York City to study at the Albany Business School and then returned to Puerto Rico to get married. In 1921 he, his wife, and their four children moved to New Jersey, where he became a broker for Spanish foods. Prudencio purchased the name Goya for $1 in 1936, and a family business was born.

That family business now has 26 facilities throughout the United States, Puerto Rico, the Dominican Republic, and Spain, and employs more than 4,500 people. "Our grandfather took a leap into the great

unknown [when he came here]," Bob said in 2016. "He was looking for a taste of home, and he also provided a taste of home for everybody else that was coming to this country."

That idea of feeling connected to community through food is an enduring part of the Latino experience in the United States. From Mexican *tamaladas* to Argentine *parrilladas*, Latinos strengthen family ties and forge bonds of friendship at food gatherings. As César Chávez put it: the people who give you their food give you their heart.

"FOOD IS A GREAT CONNECTION."

Likewise, the hard work and dedication of all family members in order to grow a business is the hallmark of immigrant entrepreneurship. Bob started working at the company when he was ten years old, packing olives in Brooklyn. He was paid fifty cents a day. Later, after the family moved to Spain when he was nineteen, Bob helped his family open the olive oil production business there. He enrolled at the University of Sevilla and learned to speak Spanish.

After finishing his studies in 1980, he became the purchasing director for Goya in Puerto Rico. He spent twenty-four years at the company in different roles and at different locations before becoming the chief executive officer in 2004. "I love to walk the production floor and talk and visit with people because their experiences, their perspectives, and the lessons I still carry from my different jobs within Goya are so valuable to me still today."

Because Latinos in the United States have high rates of diabetes and obesity, Bob stepped up when First Lady Michelle Obama asked Goya to help launch MiPlato, a national health initiative focused on food and health education for Latinxs. The company supports more than 250 nonprofits working to improve health and wellness in the Latino community and gives away millions of pounds of food through Catholic charities.

Bob, who was married for thirty years and has six children and a growing number of grandchildren, has said that family, God, and work are his touchstones—and the recipe for success in his family's business.

READING GUIDE

BY EMILY KEY,
OFFICE OF AUDIENCE ENGAGEMENT,
NATIONAL MUSEUM OF THE AMERICAN LATINO

BOOK SUMMARY

Who is Latino? What does it mean to be Latino? What is our individual and cultural identity, and how does this interact with the formation of our national identity? This book is a compilation of biographies of Latinas and Latinos who have shaped the United States and is our way of beginning to tell the complete story of our national culture and identity. Thorough research was done in selecting these individuals that represent key moments in U.S. history from the nineteenth century through present day. We may only know their names, and sometimes just a few specifics of their actions, but each of these individuals has changed the course of American history from education, fashion, civil rights, and science to arts, sports, health, and law. This selection is not the full listing of Latino impact in the United States; however, it serves as a beginner's guide to spark our collective and individual curiosity to learn more and dive deeper.

READING GUIDE

This reading guide poses critical questions to spark discussions about these individuals and various time periods in American history, while also connecting people and themes. Included is a list of additional Smithsonian resources and an online Smithsonian Learning Lab Collection for use by parents and teachers.

The Smithsonian has more than 154 million artifacts, works of art, and specimens in its collection. This includes everything from bugs to the space shuttle. These collections continue to grow and, in many cases, gaps that currently exist will be filled. Many of the Smithsonian's resources are available online. The digital Smithsonian effort includes making many of our collections searchable and available as primary source material. We have compiled a list of Smithsonian Latino resources and created a collection on the Smithsonian's Learning Lab.

Please scan the QR code (using a phone app or a phone's camera) to gain access to images, documents, and recordings that relate to our profiled Latinos in *Nuestra América*. Here, you will find collections, resources, and additional activities that relate to the anthology. You can also visit www.latino.si.edu for more information.

The Smithsonian Learning Lab Collection includes resources about:

- Celia Cruz
- Julia de Burgos
- Ellen Ochoa
- Roberto Clemente
- Lin Manuel Miranda
- C. David Molina
- Unanue Family and Goya Foods
- Sandra Cisneros
- César Chávez
- Dolores Huerta
- Sylvia Méndez
- Óscar de la Renta
- Sonia Sotomayor
- Jaime Escalante
- Pura Belpré
- Rita Moreno
- Dara Torres

The National Museum of the American Latino is the keystone to learning about Latino contributions to U.S. art, history, culture, and science. Thanks to the foundational work of the Smithsonian Latino Center and its collaborations with Smithsonian museums, the National Latino Museum has a robust program of exhibitions, public events, and research to tell the stories of Latinos in the United States. Visitors can view many of these stories in the Molina Family Latino Gallery at the National Museum of American History. To delve deeper into the stories featured here, as well as many others, please visit: www.latino.si.edu.

SELECT GLOSSARY OF TERMS

assimilate: to adjust and conform to the customs, attitudes, and ways of a specific group of people or a country

Chicana /Chicano: a chosen identity of some Mexican Americans in the United States

clinical psychologist: a person in the mental health profession who handles the diagnosis and treatment of personality or behavioral disorders

constitutionality: adhering to the constitution of a country or state

Cuban Revolution: an armed revolt conducted by Fidel Castro's revolutionary 26th of July Movement and its allies against the military dictatorship of Cuban President Fulgencio Batista. The revolution began in July 1953 and continued sporadically until the rebels finally ousted Batista on December 31, 1958, replacing his government with a revolutionary socialist state.

entrepreneurship: when a person organizes and runs their own company or business by themselves or with little help from other organizations

Fidel Castro: Cuban communist revolutionary that led Cuba from 1959 to 2008

huipiles: the most common traditional garment worn by indigenous women from central Mexico to Central America

Latinx: a gender-neutral term that is sometimes used instead of Latino or Latina. In this publication, Latinx is only used when the individual profiled has identified as such.

#MeToo Movement: the Me Too movement, with a large variety of locally and internationally related names, is a movement against sexual harassment and sexual assault

noncommissioned officer: a person enlisted in the military who holds a rank below another officer

paleontologists: someone who studies the science of different life forms, usually through fossils, from different periods in the earth's history

posthumously: being after or continuing beyond one's death

Rebozos: shawls

systems engineer: someone who specializes in discovering problems that need to be solved and then designing and managing work processes and risk management tools to solve those problems

Taíno: Arawak-speaking peoples from South America who began settling the Caribbean islands more than 2,000 years ago. Their descendants, the Taino, reside on the Greater Antilles and surrounding islands.

DISCUSSION QUESTIONS

The individuals highlighted are just some of the many Latinos that have impacted U.S. history. Discuss the meaning of *Nuestra América* (Our America) and its usage of Spanish language as a title header. What is the significance of this?

Contemplating some of the civil rights and labor leaders showcased in this anthology, what do you think are some of the commonalities and differences regarding their motivations, actions, and legacies?

Macario García is just one of many Latino patriots in American military history. What does it mean to be a patriot? Place yourself in the shoes of Macario García and others who have had to prove their loyalty and justify their belonging in the United States, despite the many heroic efforts they displayed fighting for U.S. interests in war. Discuss these situations and how one might remedy these issues. (Visit https://latino.si.edu/learn/teaching-and-learning-resources/bilingual-materials to learn more about Latino military involvement from the Revolutionary War to Vietnam.)

After reading the biographies of the Latinas who form part of this list, discuss what it means to be a double or triple minority? What actions did these women take that allowed them to make deep impacts in their communities and in U.S. history? How might young women today learn from their example?

Drawing from the anthology's artists, writers, musicians, and performers, discuss how the arts plays a role in social change throughout history.

What is the role of a library? Why are libraries important and how can we use them to transform how we learn?

Thinking about Jaime Escalante's way of teaching and his dedication to his students, discuss your favorite teacher and their impact on your studies and/or life.

What is the role of museums in telling and sharing stories to represent a community?

Thinking about history, how does science and discovery impact cultural development and representation?

Referring to the story of Xiuhtezcatl Martínez, what is the role of the individual in conservation efforts? What kinds of projects are important and/or unique that community members should undertake? What and/or how can we as community members contribute?

Many of the athletes highlighted in this anthology spent years working on their craft. Discuss the role of dedication and perseverance in becoming a leader.

Fairness, justice, and rights are all themes that come up throughout this anthology. Looking at the way César Chávez, Dolores Huerta, Sylvia Méndez, Sylvia Rivera, and Sonia Sotomayor apply these terms in their individual and collective efforts, what is the role of the United States Constitution in aiding this effort? How have the laws of the land been interpreted, changed, or reconceived by these individuals and their actions?

The realities of the Mexican-American and Puerto Rican community in the contemporary United States are direct results of two wars that changed the geographic landscape and people of America. Research general information about the cause, actions, and effects of the Mexican-American War in 1845 and the Spanish-American War in 1898. Create a list of consequences from the results of these wars. Can you identify how some of the people that are featured in this anthology were or currently are affected by these results?

Entrepreneurs like C. David Molina and Robert Unanue are critical to the success of the United States. Entrepreneurs look at what society needs and create opportunities for these needs to be met through innovation, creativity, and problem-solving. Think about a need in your community and propose a solution to that problem.

After reading this anthology, reflect on and discuss this statement: Latinos were, are, and will continue to be a part of the American story.

Using a newspaper- or reporter-writing style, construct an article, blog, or social media video series about one or a group of the Latinos profiled in this book and the message that their impact shared. Connect their efforts with a current event in the news or in your community.